HOW TO BECOME A REBEL

A long time ago, the evil Empire instilled fear throughout the entire galaxy. Only the Rebel Alliance could stop the menace of the Imperial forces. The rebel leaders took every opportunity to recruit brave new heroes into their ranks.

MISSING DROIDS

At their base on Yavin 4, the rebels are preparing for battle with the Empire. Help them get ready for their mission by finding the four astromech droids hidden in this picture.

R2-A5

R5-D4

R2-D2

R3-A2

REBEL TRAINING

Princess Leia is teaching the new recruits how to spot friend from foe in the dark. Match the shadows to each character by writing the correct letters in the empty circles.

THIS GOLDEN DROID LOOKS FAMILIAR...

IT'S THE INFAMOUS SEE-THREEPIO. HAVEN'T YOU HEARD ABOUT HIS 'PERFECT LANDING' ON TATOOINE?

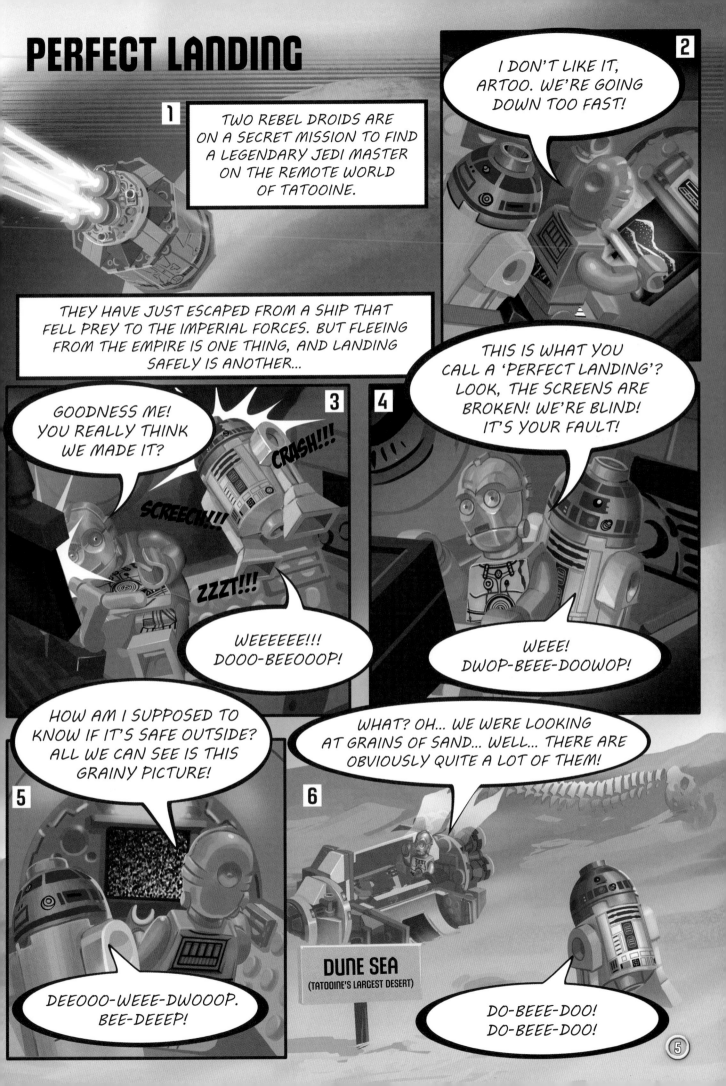

ATTACK ON THE DEATH STAR

The rebels are attacking the Death Star! Help them locate the position of all the defending TIE fighters using the grid opposite. The TIEs can only appear once in each row or column.

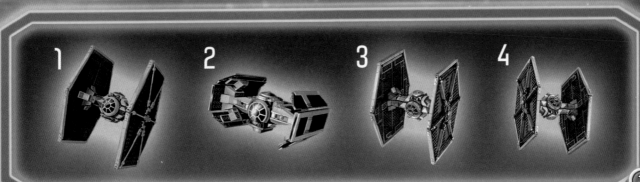

REBELS IN THE SNOW

Heavy snowfall has blocked the way to the rebel snowspeeders on planet Hoth. Guide these two pilots through the snowy maze, steering clear of the hungry wampas.

FINISH

SELFIE WITH THE HERO

The Freemakers - a family of brave scavengers - found their new home in the Rebel Alliance's flagship, *Home One*. They were very happy to see the Rebellion's greatest hero, Luke Skywalker, again.

Take a close look at Luke. The next time you see him in this book, he'll be much older (and hooded). Now, look carefully at the two photos taken by Roger, the family's butler droid, and circle eight differences between them.

MAGNET FOR TROUBLE

Roger, the Freemakers' butler droid, is very good at getting into trouble. Luke finds the stories of Roger's epic fails very amusing. Match the stories with the pictures by writing the correct numbers in the empty boxes.

1 DO YOU REMEMBER WHEN I TOLD ROGER TO CLEAN A CLIENT'S SHIP? WHEN I SAW HE HAD TAKEN IT APART, HE SAID HE'D MADE EVERY BRICK LOOK LIKE NEW!

2 YEAH! WHAT ABOUT WHEN HE FOUND THAT IMPERIAL WALKER STANDING AT THE EDGE OF A CLIFF? FIRST WE HEARD ROGER'S HAPPY VOICE AND THEN THE SOUND OF CRASHING METAL! LATER HE EXPLAINED HE'D BARELY TOUCHED THE WALKER.

3 HMM... I ONCE SPENT ALL DAY LOOKING FOR A PART THAT ROGER HAD ACCIDENTALLY LOST. HE JUST COULDN'T STAND STILL AND KEPT BUMPING AGAINST EVERY WALL ON OUR SHIP.

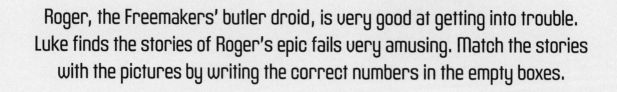

A

B

C

LOST IN *HOME ONE*

The Freemakers need some rest after a long and exciting day. Unfortunately, they got lost on their way to their cabins. Help them choose the correct path to the crew deck door. (Clue: it's the one with the largest sum of all the numbers on it.)

CABIN NUMBER

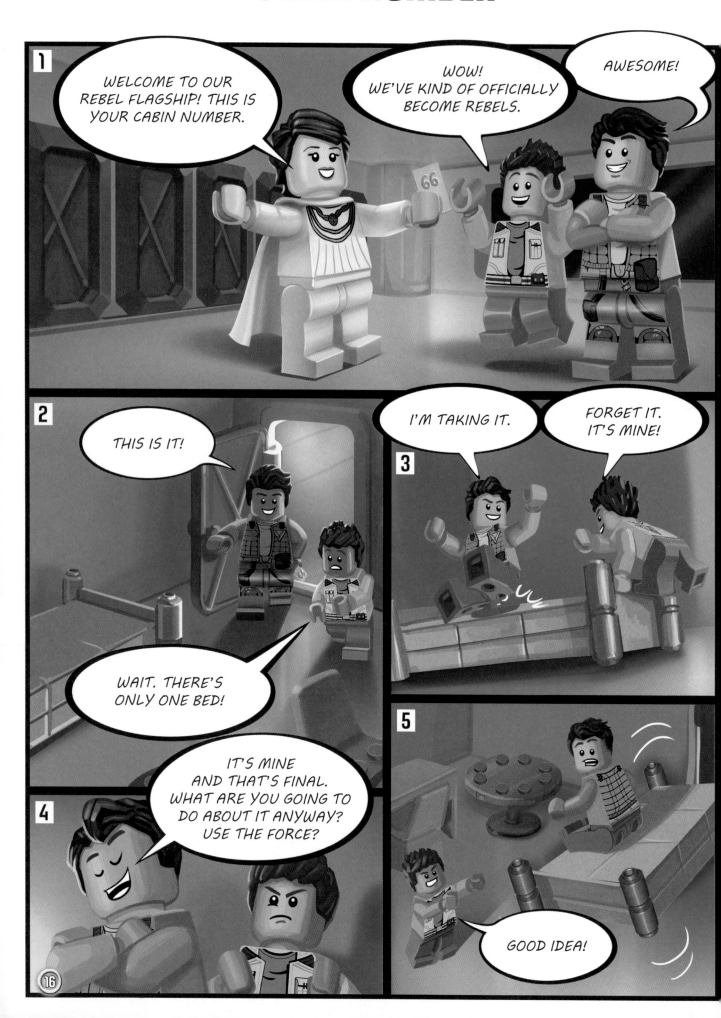

THE BEST PILOTS

Luke Skywalker and Wedge Antilles are fighting a space battle with the Imperial TIE fighters. All the young rebel pilots want to learn their tricks. Can you locate the two pilots' X-wings in the picture?

LUKE SKYWALKER

WEDGE ANTILLES

DEATH STAR TOUR

It's your last opportunity to see what's inside the second Death Star before the rebels blow it up! Visit every point of interest, from points A to F. Make sure you don't stumble on any of the Imperial stormtroopers!

START

A

WHICH IS MINE?

Poe Dameron, the best pilot in the Resistance, is confused. There is an almost identical X-wing fighter next to his, but it's missing one small detail. Can you tell which X-wing belongs to Poe by finding the one with the missing part?

OH, COME ON, GUYS! I'M IN A HURRY... I NEED TO SAVE THE GALAXY!

Now that you know which part of the X-wing fighter is missing, finding it shouldn't be a problem. A smart rebel needs less than 30 seconds to spot it in the picture. How fast can you do it?

THE DUEL

Kylo Ren cannot bear the thought of Rey being as strong with the Force as he is. The only way to solve this is with a lightsaber duel. Help Rey choose the right strikes to defend herself against her opponent's attacks.

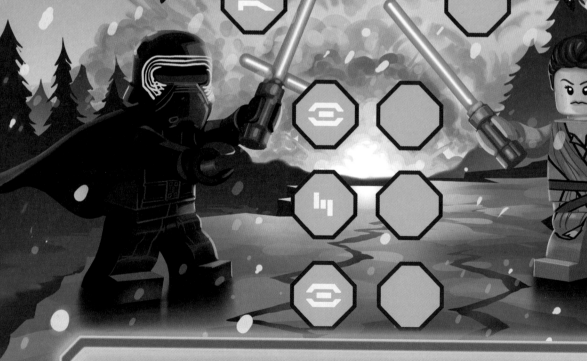

ATTACKS:

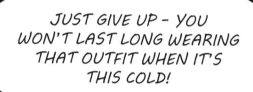 forward strike	

forward strike

cut from the left

cut from the right

DEFENCE:

block the cut from the right **A**

block the forward strike **B**

block the cut from the left **C**

CHEWIE TO THE RESCUE

The entire planet is falling apart, so Rey and Finn need help. Luckily, Chewbacca is looking for them in the *Millennium Falcon*. Find where the young heroes are and write their coordinates in the box.

WRITE THE COORDINATES HERE:

MEETING THE LEGEND

Soon after defeating Kylo Ren and destroying the First Order's Starkiller base, Rey arrived on planet Ahch-To to finally meet with the legendary Jedi Master Luke Skywalker and hand him his very own lightsaber.

YOU'VE COME TO THE WRONG PLACE. WHATEVER YOU'RE SELLING – I DON'T WANT IT!

The old hero of the Rebellion has lived on the planet Ahch-To for a very long time and he does not like unexpected guests - neither do the porgs. How many of those skittish creatures are hiding in the scene?

=

STAR QUIZ

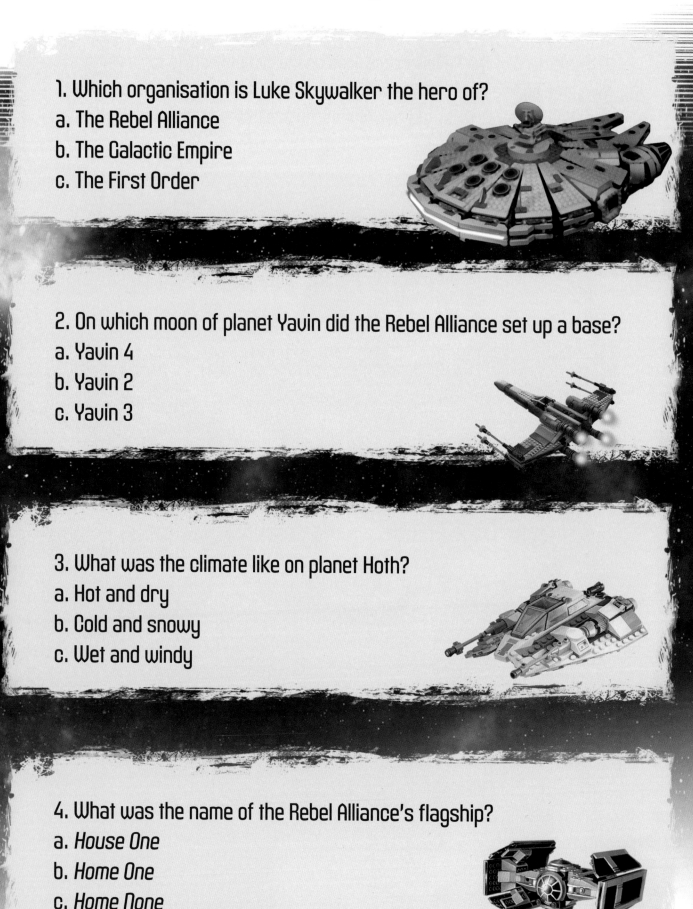

1. Which organisation is Luke Skywalker the hero of?
a. The Rebel Alliance
b. The Galactic Empire
c. The First Order

2. On which moon of planet Yavin did the Rebel Alliance set up a base?
a. Yavin 4
b. Yavin 2
c. Yavin 3

3. What was the climate like on planet Hoth?
a. Hot and dry
b. Cold and snowy
c. Wet and windy

4. What was the name of the Rebel Alliance's flagship?
a. *House One*
b. *Home One*
c. *Home None*

5. What was the Freemakers' butler droid good at?
a. Building starships
b. Getting into trouble
c. Getting out of trouble

6. What was the name of the best pilot in the Resistance?
a. Pol Dameron
b. Pod Lameron
c. Poe Dameron

7. On what planet did Rey find the legendary Luke Skywalker?
a. Ah-Choo
b. Ahch-To
c. Ah-Too

WHY IS HE SO ANGRY?

HE WANTED THE LAST QUESTION TO BE ABOUT HIM, BUT IT'S ABOUT LUKE SKYWALKER!

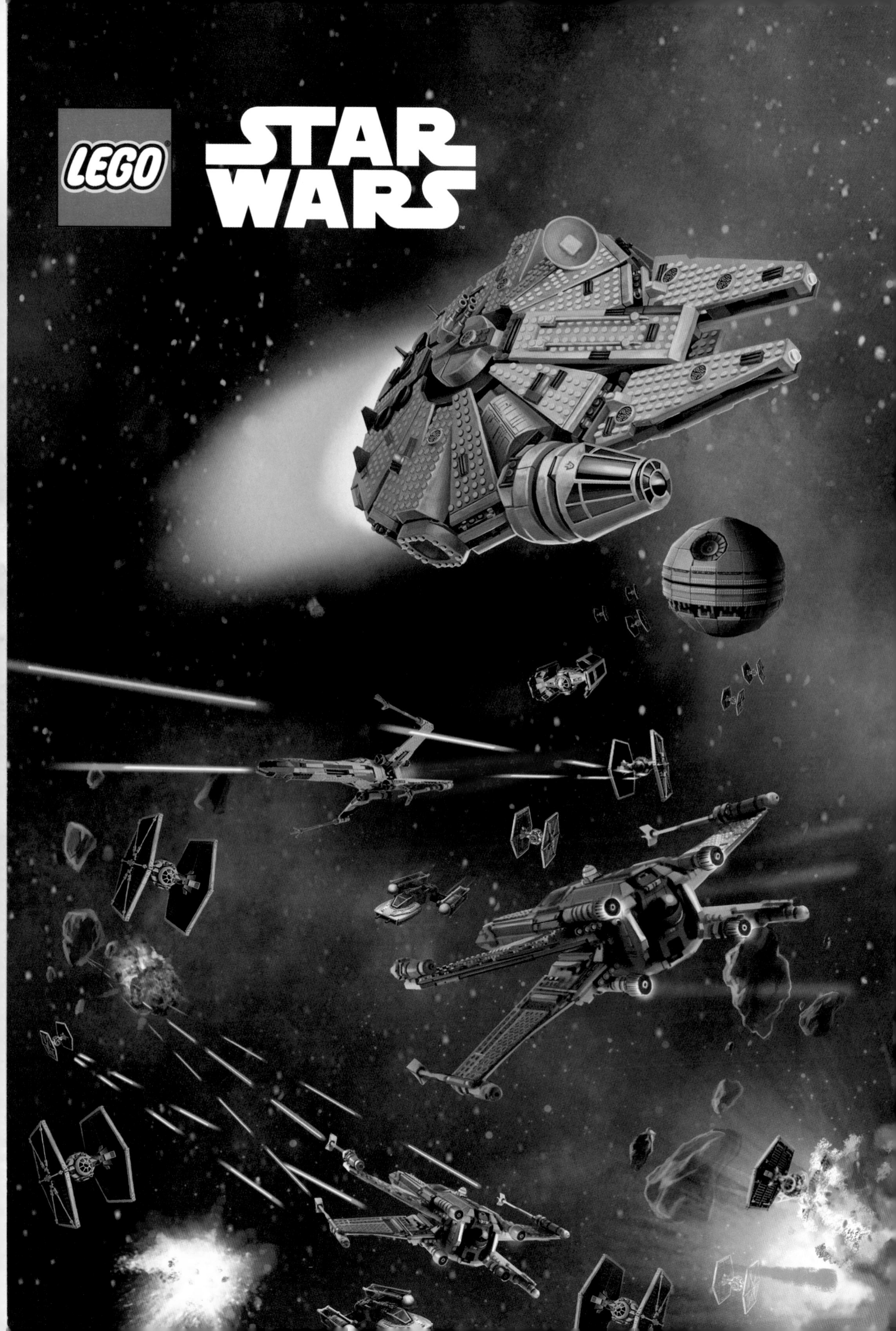
LEGO
STAR WARS